A MONEY MATTERS GUIDE

Pay by Check

a guide to checking accounts

JANIS FISHER CHAN

GLOBE FEARON

MONEY MATTERS GUIDES

Master Your Money
A Guide to Budgeting

Make Your Money Grow
A Guide to Savings Plans

Pay by Check
A Guide to Checking Accounts

Insure Yourself
A Guide to Insurance

More for Your Money
A Guide to Comparison Shopping

Be Credit-Wise
A Guide to Credit

Be Ad-Wise
A Guide to Reading Ads

Know Your Rights
A Guide to Consumer Protection

PROJECT REVISION TEAM
Editorial Consultant: Stuart E. Schwartz
Content Editor: Craig A. Conley
Executive Editor: Joan Carrafiello
Designer: Pencil Point Studio
Cover Designer: Pencil Point Studio
Production Editor: Rosann Bar
Marketing Manager: Margaret Rakus

Printed in the United States of America
1 2 3 4 5 6 7 8 9 10 99 98 97 96

ISBN: 0-8359-3324-5
B-88

GLOBE FEARON EDUCATIONAL PUBLISHER
A Division of Simon & Schuster
Upper Saddle River, New Jersey

Contents ....

Introduction

Have you ever watched someone write a check to pay for something? Did you wonder how a person can pay with a piece of paper instead of cash? That person has a checking account.

A checking account is a special kind of bank account. If you keep your money in a checking account, you can use checks instead of cash when you buy certain things. Checks are another form of cash.

Checks are safer than cash. If you lose cash, anyone can spend it. But only *you* can spend your checks. A checking account also makes it easy to keep track of your money.

In this book, you will learn how you can open a checking account. You will also learn how to write checks. And you will learn how using a checking account can help you spend your money wisely.

Why Use Checks?

Alfredo has two jobs. On Saturdays, he helps Mr. Nito at the grocery store. After school, he works at a day-care center. He works hard for his money.

Alfredo keeps his money in a shoe box under his bed. When he needs cash, he takes it out of the box.

One day, he decides to take out $35.00 to fix his motorcycle.

"Hey, Ted!" he says to his friend. "Look at this. I have only $15.00 left. I had $50.00 the last time I counted."

"Did you buy anything since then?" Ted asks.

Alfredo thinks for a minute. "Well, a few things, I guess. A new shirt and a birthday gift for my mom. Oh, and I took Sheila to the movies last night."

"That's where your money went," Ted says. "Why do you keep it in a shoe box anyhow? No wonder you can't keep track of your money. Besides, cash can get stolen if you keep it around the house."

Where do you keep your money?

_____

_____

KEEPING MONEY SAFE

The safest place to keep your money is in a bank, savings and loan, or a credit union. In this book, we will use the word "bank" to mean any of these. When you put money in a bank, you get your own account. There are two kinds of accounts. One is called a savings account. The other is called a checking account.

A **savings account** is for money you don't want to spend right away. To save for something that costs a lot, you put your money in a savings account.

A **checking account** is for money you might want to spend soon. You put that money into your checking account. You can write checks for as much money as you put in. The checks are just as good as coins and bills. But checks are safer than cash.

PUZZLER

Look in the box for the word that belongs in each blank.
Then write in your answer.

1. A _____ is the safest place to keep your money.

2. _____ can get stolen too easily.

3. You can put money that you want to spend soon in a
   _____ account.

4. You can use _____ the same way you use cash.

> cash
>
> bank
>
> checks
>
> checking

WHY CHECKS ARE SAFER THAN CASH

A **check** is a piece of paper from the bank that you write on. The check tells your bank to pay someone money from your account.

But people at the bank won't pay until they make sure that you are the one who signed the check.

No one else can buy things with your checks. When you pay by check at a store, you have to prove that you're the person who has the checking account.

If you lose cash, anyone can spend it. But only you can buy things with your checks.

HOW CHECKS HELP KEEP TRACK OF MONEY

Alfredo's friend Ted has a checking account. In his checkbook, Ted keeps a list of the amounts of money he puts into the account. He also keeps a record of the checks he writes.

The record in the checkbook helps Ted keep track of the way he spends his money.

In *Pay by Check*, you will learn how to open and use a checking account. Then you can keep track of your money—and keep your money safe!

PUZZLE TIME

Decide what word belongs in each blank. Then find and circle that word in the puzzle. The answers are printed across, down, up, backwards, and on a slant. The answer to number 1 is circled for you.

1. Anyone can spend _____.

2. Only you can _____ things with your checks.

3. A _____ is a piece of paper from your bank that tells the bank to pay someone money from your account.

4. You keep a record of the amounts you put into your checking _____.

5. You keep a record of the checks you _____.

6. Your record will help you keep track of the way you _____ your money.

```
A  C  A  S  H  B  C  S
D  E  F  G  H  I  J  P
K  L  K  C  E  H  C  E
M  B  N  O  P  Q  A  N
R  S  U  T  U  C  V  D
W  X  Y  Y  C  E  Z  A
B  C  D  O  E  T  F  G
H  I  U  J  K  I  L  M
N  N  O  P  Q  R  R  S
T  T  U  V  W  W  X  Y
```

Unit 2

Opening a Checking Account

Tracy wants to open a checking account. She looks around the bank. On a desk near the door she spots a sign that says, "New Accounts."

As Tracy walks up to the desk, the woman behind it looks up and smiles. "Is this where I open a checking account?" Tracy asks.

"That's right," says the woman. "I'm Ms. Lee. I'll be happy to help you."

What if Tracy had not spotted the New Accounts sign? How could she find out what to do?

_____

_____

Tracy could ask anyone who works in the bank.

 THE SIGNATURE CARD

"The first step in opening a checking account is filling out a form called the signature card," Ms. Lee explains.

"Your **signature** is your name in your own handwriting. You sign your name on the card the same way you will sign your checks. When we want to see if the signature on a check is really yours, we match it to the one on the card."

WHAT THE BANK NEEDS TO KNOW

You write more than your signature on the card. When you open a checking account, the bank needs to know some things about you.

"We need to know how to reach you by mail and by phone," Ms. Lee tells Tracy. "We also need information showing that your account belongs to you, not to someone with a name like yours."

Part of Tracy's signature card is shown below. Ms. Lee helped Tracy find the right place to write in each of these things:

1. The address where Tracy gets her mail

2. Her phone number at home

3. Her phone number at work

4. The day, month, and year she was born

5. The name of the city where she was born

Each box next to the signature card has an arrow pointing to one of the kinds of information listed above. Write each number from the list in the matching circle. The first one is done for you.

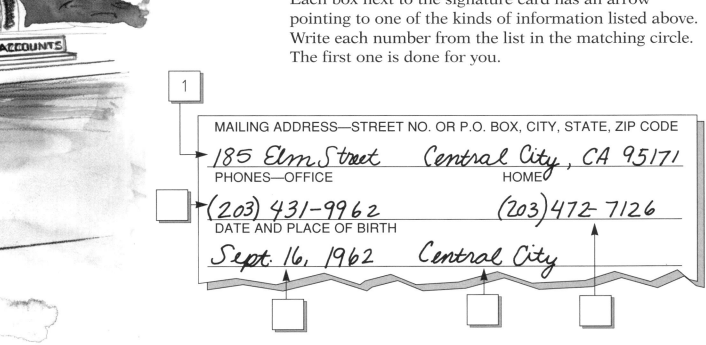

1

MAILING ADDRESS—STREET NO. OR P.O. BOX, CITY, STATE, ZIP CODE

185 Elm Street   Central City, CA 95171

PHONES—OFFICE   HOME

(203) 431-9962   (203) 472-7126

DATE AND PLACE OF BIRTH

Sept. 16, 1962   Central City

MOTHER'S MAIDEN NAME

When you cash a check, the bank needs to make sure that you are the person named on the account. On the signature card, you write the answer to a question that only *you* can answer: What is your mother's maiden name?

A woman's **maiden name** is her family name when she is born.

What is your mother's maiden name?

_____

When people at the bank want to make sure you are who you say you are, they ask what your mother's maiden name is. Someone pretending to be you couldn't answer that question; so he or she couldn't take money out of your account.

SOCIAL SECURITY NUMBER

The bank has another way of knowing that your account belongs to you. You will be asked to write your Social Security number on the signature card.

Do you have a Social Security card?

    Yes   No

If you answered yes, write your Social Security number here.

_____

12

■ EMPLOYER

There's a place on your signature card to write in the name of your **employer**. Your employer is the person or company you work for.

There's also a place on the signature card to write in the kind of job you have.

You can see part of Tracy's signature card below. Ms. Lee showed Tracy where to write in each of these things:

1. Her mother's maiden, or birth name

2. Her Social Security number

3. Where she works and the kind of job she has

Match each kind of information in the list with its place on Tracy's signature card. Write each number in the matching box.

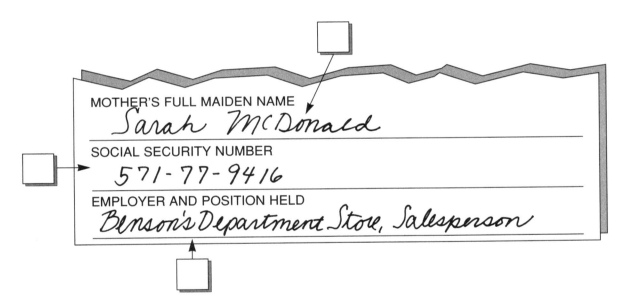

MOTHER'S FULL MAIDEN NAME
Sarah McDonald

SOCIAL SECURITY NUMBER
571-77-9416

EMPLOYER AND POSITION HELD
Benson's Department Store, Salesperson

Now, you try. Suppose that you have a job. Write these things in the signature card below.

1. Your mailing address

2. Your work phone number

3. Your home phone number

4. Your date and place of birth

5. Your mother's maiden name, or birth name

6. Your Social Security number

7. Your employer and the kind of job you have

MAILING ADDRESS—STREET NO. OR P.O. BOX, CITY, STATE, ZIP CODE

_____

PHONES—OFFICE   HOME
(   )   (   )

DATE AND PLACE OF BIRTH

_____

MOTHER'S FULL MAIDEN NAME

_____

SOCIAL SECURITY NO.

_____

EMPLOYER AND POSITION HELD

_____

SIGNING A CONTRACT

. . . .

The signature card is a **contract**, or agreement, between you and the bank. When you sign the card, you agree to follow the bank's rules. The bank agrees to give you certain services.

One rule you agree to is not to write a check unless you have enough money in your account to pay it. There are other rules too. Ask the person who helps you open your account what they are. Always know what you agree to when you sign a contract.

Ms. Lee shows Tracy where to sign the card. She says, "Always sign your checks the same way you signed this card."

Tracy signs her name this way.

Tracy Ann Johnson

"You wrote your middle name, Ann, on this card," Ms. Lee says. "The signature on your checks should match."

PUZZLE TIME

Look in the box for the word that belongs in each sentence clue. Then, write in your answer. Use your answers to complete the crossword puzzle.

employer
signature
maiden
information
contract
name
number

Down

1. The first step in opening a checking account is filling out

   a _____ card.

2. The signature card is a _____,
   or agreement.

4. To make sure you are who you say you are, someone will

   ask you what your mother's _____ name is.

6. There is a place on the card for your Social Security _____.

Across

3. The bank needs _____ showing that your account
   belongs to you.

5. Your signature is your _____ in your own handwriting.

7. The person or company you work for is your _____.

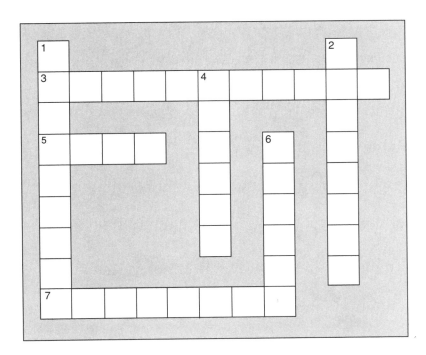

Unit 3

Which Bank Is Best?

• •

Jason is a smart shopper. When he buys something, he tries to find the best deal. To find a good used car, he shopped around and bought the best car he could find at the lowest price.

Before Jason opened a checking account, what do you think he did?

_____

_____

_____

Of course! He shopped around to find the best bank.

Banks offer many kinds of services. They lend money for things like cars and houses. They rent safe places to keep important papers. They also offer savings and checking accounts.

Different banks charge different prices for the same service. Jason looked for the best service at the lowest price.

To choose a bank, you may want to ask about several services. In this book, we're going to talk only about checking accounts.

KINDS OF CHECKING ACCOUNTS

Most banks offer three or four kinds of checking accounts. You will probably want to get regular or special checking.

Regular checking is best if you write ten or more checks every month. Most banks charge a few dollars each month for the account and a certain amount for each check you write. At some banks, there are no charges if you keep a certain amount in your account.

Special checking is best if you write less than ten checks every month. There's no monthly charge. You pay a charge only for the checks you write. The cost is different from bank to bank.

Jason thinks he will probably write about seven checks every month. What type of checking account should he get? Circle your answer.

       Regular   Special

Jason decides that a special checking account will be cheaper for him.

 ## FINDING THE BEST DEAL

Jason looks at the cost of special checking account at three banks. This is what he finds.

Special Checking			
	Main Street Bank	National Bank	Garberville Bank
Monthly charge	None	None	None
Cost for writing each check	$ .70	$ .65	$ .65 for the first five $ .70 for every check after five

Which bank has the lowest price?

    Main Street   National   Garberville

National Bank has the lowest price.

OTHER THINGS TO LOOK FOR

The cost of writing checks is only one thing to look for. Jason thought about these things too:

Statements—A statement is a list of all the checks you write, the money you put into your account, and the bank's charges. Some banks send a statement every month. Others send statements every three months.

Bank-by-Mail—Some banks have a plan for putting money in your account by mail. That saves you trips to the bank.

Branches—A branch is an office of the bank. If the bank has many branches, it's easy to find one near your home or place of work.

Minimum Deposit—Each time you add money to your account, you make a deposit. The *least* amount of money that you can deposit in a bank to open your account is that bank's *minimum* deposit. Many banks have a rule that you must deposit at least $50.00 or $100.00 to open a checking account. Other banks let you open an account with as little as $5.00.

Jason compares the services at three banks. Here's what he finds.

	National Bank	Garberville Bank	Main Street Bank
Monthly statements?	Yes	Yes	No
Bank-by-Mail?	Yes	Yes	No
Many Branches?	Yes	No	Yes
Minimum Deposit?	$50.00	$100.00	$100.00

Which bank do you think has the best deal?

   National   Garberville   Main Street

Jason chooses *National Bank.*

PUZZLE TIME

Look in the box for the word that belongs in each numbered sentence. Then, write that word in the puzzle next to the matching number. The first one is done for you.

1. Shop for the bank with the best _____ at the lowest prices.

2. _____ checking is best if you write ten or more checks every month.

3. Suppose you write less than ten checks a month. You will save money by getting a _____ checking account.

4. The minimum _____ is the least amount of money you can put in the bank to open your account.

5. You will want to choose a bank with a branch _____ to your house or place of work.

| close |
| regular |
| deposit |
| services |
| special |

1. _s_ _e_ _r_ _v_ _i_ _c_ _e_ _s_

2. __ _e_ __ __ __ __ __

3. __ __ _e_ __ __ __ __

4. __ _e_ __ __ __ __ __

5. __ __ __ __ _e_

Making a Deposit

Anita is making a **deposit**. That means she's putting money into her account.

First, she takes a deposit slip out of her checkbook. It looks like this.

PARKTOWN BANK			Dollars	Cents
Parktown, PA 19000	CASH	Currency		
		Coin		
Date _____ 19__	List Checks Separately			
Sign here if cash received from deposit				
_____	TOTAL			
Anita D. Gomez	Less Cash			
475 Miller Ave.	Net Deposit			
Parktown, PA 19001				
30900086 2880 081186858 4733				

You can find the answers to these questions on Anita's deposit slip.

1. What is the name of Anita's bank?

   _____

   Anita uses the Parktown Bank.

2. What street does Anita live on?

   _____

   She lives on Miller Ave.

3. What do you think the long number at the bottom of the deposit slip is used for?

   _____

   It's Anita's account number. Each person has his or her own account number

4. What word from the deposit slip belongs in the blank under the picture of the metal money?

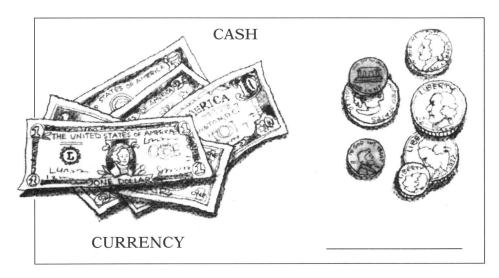

CASH

CURRENCY   _____

Coin is the answer.

5. The deposit slip has a place to list checks *one at a time*. It says,

   "List checks _____*."*

   Separately means "one at a time."

FILLING OUT A DEPOSIT SLIP

Anita wants to deposit the cash and the two checks shown below.

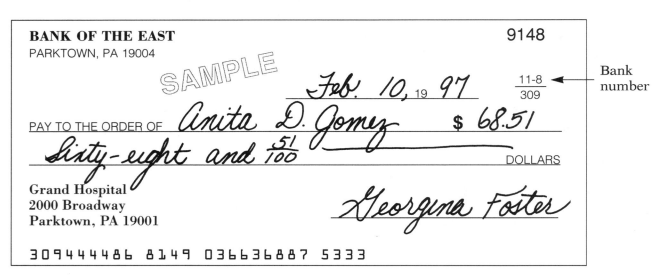

BANK OF THE EAST   9148
PARKTOWN, PA 19004

SAMPLE

Feb. 10, 19 97   11-8 / 309 ← Bank number

PAY TO THE ORDER OF _Anita D. Gomez_ $ 68.51

Sixty-eight and 51/100   DOLLARS

Grand Hospital
2000 Broadway
Parktown, PA 19001

Georgina Foster

⑆309444486 8149 036636887 5333

FARMERS BANK   3147
LAWRENCE, KS 66044

SAMPLE

Feb. 17 19 97   3-5 / 309 ← Bank number

PAY TO THE ORDER OF _Anita Gomez_ $ 20.00

Twenty and XX/100   DOLLARS

Joseph Saul
590 Dover Square
Lawrence, KS 66044

Joseph Saul

⑆428100291 4147 041436859 8888

Anita is ready to fill out the deposit slip shown at the bottom of this page.

First, she writes in the date—**February 18, 1997.** Find the line marked *Date* on the deposit slip.

Write **February 18** on the line.

Now, write 97 after the 19.

Next, Anita writes in the amount of paper money she wants to deposit. Paper money is called currency. How much currency is shown on page 22?

$_____

Anita is depositing $12.00 in paper money, or currency. That amount is already written in for you. Find it on the deposit slip. It's next to the word *Currency*.

How much is Anita depositing in coins?

$_____

$2.60 is the amount that should be written next to the word *Coin*. Write the **2** in the *Dollars* column. Write the **60** in the *Cents* column.

Anita lists each check by bank number. Look at the top check on page 22. The bank number is marked with an arrow and a box.

Now, find that bank number on Anita's deposit slip. Next to 11-8, write the amount of the check—**$68.51.** Put the **68** in the *Dollars* column. Put the **51** in the *Cents* column.

Find the bank number of the $20.00 check. Write it on the deposit slip under the other bank number.

The bank number on the $20.00 check is **3-5.**

How much is Anita depositing all together? To find out, add the amounts of the cash and the checks. Write the answer next to the words *Total deposit*.

Anita is depositing $103.11 all together.

PARKTOWN BANK			Dollars	Cents
Parktown, PA 19000	CASH	Currency	12	00
		Coin		
Date _____ 19__	List Check Separately			
		11-8		
Sign here if cash received from deposit			20	00
_____	TOTAL			
Anita D. Gomez	Less Cash			
475 Miller Ave.	Net Deposit			
Parktown, PA 19001				

30900086 2880 081186858 4733

ENDORSING CHECKS

Anita's deposit slip is filled out. Now she is ready to **endorse** her checks. That means she is ready to sign her name on the bank of each check.

Anita does not endorse her checks until she gets to the bank. She wants to make sure that she doesn't lose endorsed checks. Once checks are endorsed, anyone can cash them.

One of her checks is made out to Anita D. Gomez. She endorses the check the same way. That endorsed check is the top one at the right.

The other check is made out to Anita Gomez, without the **D.** Anita usually signs things with the **D.** Anita knows that whenever her name on a check is different from the way she usually signs things, she needs to sign her name two times.

First, she writes her name the way it appears on the front of the check. Then she writes it the way she usually signs things. That endorsed check is the bottom one at the right.

Endorse Here

X _Anita D. Gomez_

_____

_____

(do not write below this line)

Endorse Here

X _Anita Gomez_
  Anita D. Gomez

_____

(do not write below this line)

TO THE TELLER

Anita takes her deposit slip, the cash, and the checks to a person behind the long counter. That person is called a bank **teller**.

The teller makes sure that Anita's deposit slip is filled out correctly. She also checks to see if Anita endorsed the checks. Then the teller gives Anita a receipt for the amount of the deposit.

When Anita makes a deposit, she brings her checkbook record up to date. Later, you will learn how to keep your own checkbook record up to date.

PUZZLE TIME

Here are eight words that you need to know to make a deposit. But the letters in each word are all mixed up. Use the clue under each word to help unscramble the letters. Then, write the word on the line.

If you need an extra clue, look at the words in the box.

Number 1 is done for you.

1. s t o p d e i _____ *deposit* _____

   An amount of money you put into your bank account

2. r e n c y c u r _____

   Paper money

3. n i o c _____

   Metal money, like pennies, nickels, dimes, and quarters

4. s h c a _____

   Money: both currency and coin

5. r s p e a t a y e l _____

   One at a time, the way you list checks on a deposit slip

6. t a d e _____

   The day, month, and year

7. s e e n d o r _____

   Sign the back of a check

8. e e l l t r _____

   Person at the bank who handles deposits

cash
coin
date
teller
deposit
endorse
currency
separately

Writing Checks

This is a big day for Jenny Fong. She has saved up enough money to buy new rollerblades. To pay for them, she is going to write a check.

Here are the things that Jenny writes on her check.

1. The date

2. The name of the store

3. The amount of money in numbers

4. The amount of money in words and numbers

5. Her signature

Where are each of those things on the check below? Match each kind of information in the list with its place on the check. Write each number in the matching box.

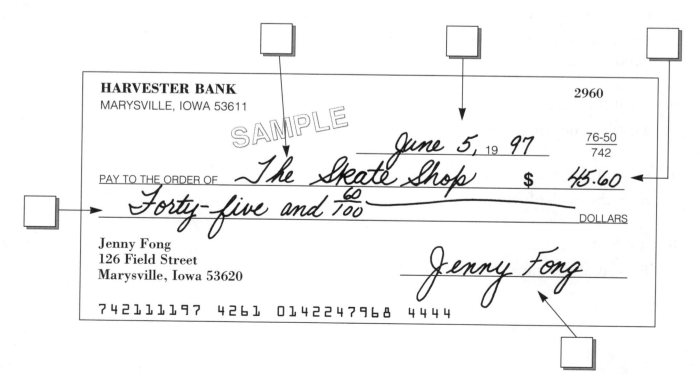

The first thing Jenny writes on the check is the date. She writes the day, the month, and the year she buys the skates.

The first two numbers of the year—19—were already printed on Jenny's check. Suppose you were writing a check today. Write today's date here.

_____ 19_____

The next thing Jenny writes on the check is the name of the store where she buys the skates. She writes it on a line marked *Pay to the order of.* That tells Jenny's bank to pay to *The Skate Shop* the amount that Jenny writes on the check—$45.60.

Where do you think the bank will get the money to pay for Jenny's skates?

_____

_____

The bank will take the $45.60 out of Jenny's checking account.

WRITING AMOUNTS ON CHECKS

On her check, Jenny writes the amount of money she's paying for the skates. She writes the amount in two ways, in numbers and in words.

Look at Jenny's check below. Find the numbers after the dollar sign, $. How does Jenny write the amount in numbers?

$_____

She writes **$45.60.**

Jenny writes the amount in words and numbers on the line marked *Dollars* at the end. First, she writes the dollars in words. How does she write **45** in words?

_____

She writes **Forty-five.** Then, she writes the word *and*. How does Jenny write the **60 cents** after the word and?

_____

She writes $\frac{60}{100}$. There are 100 cents in one dollar.

$\frac{60}{100n}$ means "60 cents out of 100 cents."

Jenny draws a line between the $\frac{60}{100}$ and the word *Dollars*.

That way, no one can write in extra words to change the amount.

HARVESTER BANK   2960
MARYSVILLE, IOWA 53611

SAMPLE

June 5, 19 97 $\frac{76-50}{742}$

PAY TO THE ORDER OF *The Skate Shop* $ 45.60

Forty-five and $\frac{60}{100}$ _____ DOLLARS

Jenny Fong
126 Field Street
Marysville, Iowa 53620   *Jenny Fong*

⑆742111197⑆ 4261 0142247968 4444

THINGS TO REMEMBER

. . . .

Jenny was going to write her check with a pencil. But the salesperson explained that it's safer to use a pen.

"Pencil marks can be erased too easily," he said. "A person could write in any amount. Always use a pen. And be sure to sign your checks."

IT'S YOUR TURN

. . . .

Suppose you are buying a CD.

It's January 10, 1997.

You're in a music store called *Disc Delight*.

The CD costs $12.95.

Fill in the check below. Remember to use a pen. And don't forget to put your signature on the bottom line.

CENTRAL BANK	112
Central City, CA 94321	

SAMPLE

19 _____   70-50 / 22

PAY TO THE ORDER OF _____ $ _____

_____ DOLLARS

YOUR NAME
YOUR ADDRESS   _____

123 456 789 0000

HELPFUL HINTS

A Suppose you were writing a check for $6.00. You could write the amount this way:

Six and $\frac{00}{100}$ ——————————— DOLLARS

But someone could change the **00** to **66** or **99**.
$\frac{00}{100}$ $\frac{66}{100}$ $\frac{99}{100}$

It's safer to write zero cents like this: **no** or **xx**
$\frac{no}{100}$ $\frac{xx}{100}$

Try writing these amounts in words and numbers. The words you will need are in the box at the right. The first one is done for you.

1. $23.00 *Twenty-three and $\frac{xx}{100}$*

2. $59.00 _____

3. $14.00 _____

4. $8.00 _____

5. $9.75 _____

6. $86.42 _____

fourteen
twenty-three
eighty-six
fifty-nine
nine
eight

B Some months have long names. You may not be able to write the whole name in the space on the check. To save space, just abbreviate the month.

Here are the short forms for the months that have long names.

January—Jan.   October—Oct.

February—Feb.   November—Nov.

August—Aug.   December—Dec.

September—Sept.

• •

Suppose you are buying a shirt.	Suppose you are getting your car fixed.
It's August 15, 1997.	It's November 9, 1997.
You're in a store called *The Clothes Horse*.	You're in a garage called *Bob's Auto*.
The shirt costs $22.00.	The repairs cost $36.54.
Fill in check number **1** below.	Fill in check number **2** below.

1

CENTRAL BANK   113
Central City, CA 94321

SAMPLE

                                                      19 _____   70-50
                                                                            22

PAY TO THE ORDER OF _____ $ _____

_____ DOLLARS

YOUR NAME
YOUR ADDRESS

123 456 789 0000

2

CENTRAL BANK   114
Central City, CA 94321

SAMPLE

                                                      19 _____   70-50
                                                                            22

PAY TO THE ORDER OF _____ $ _____

_____ DOLLARS

YOUR NAME
YOUR ADDRESS

123 456 789 0000

REVIEW PUZZLE

Look in the box on page 33 for the word that belongs in each sentence clue. Then, write in your answer. Use your answers to complete the crossword puzzle.

Down

1. When you sign a signature card, you _____ not to write checks for more money than you have in your account.

2. Your signature is your _____ in your own handwriting.

3. Shop for the bank with the best _____ at the lowest prices.

4. A _____ is a piece of paper from your bank that tells the bank to pay someone money from your account.

6. To put money into your account, you fill out a

   _____ slip.

8. Use a _____ to write checks.

Across

3. The first step in opening a checking account is filling out a

   _____ card.

5. To _____ a check means to sign it on the back.

7. *Pay to the order of* tells your bank to

   _____ someone out of your account.

9. A _____ at the bank will help you with your deposit.

services   signature   deposit
pen   check   endorse
teller   pay   name
agree

Unit 6

Keeping Track of Your Money

Linda has a date for the big school dance. She wants to buy a new dress. To see if she has enough money, she looks in her checkbook **register**. She turns to the last page that has writing on it. This is what she sees.

CHECK NUMBER	DATE	DESCRIPTION	AMOUNT OF WITHDRAWAL		AMOUNT OF DEPOSIT		BALANCE	
							$ 83	20
006	May 19,	Discount Village	$ 25	00	$		-25	00
	1997	radio					58	20

The amount left in Linda's checking account is called her account **balance**. Linda's balance right now is the *last* number in the register column marked *Balance*.

What is Linda's balance? $_____

Linda has $58.20 left in her account.

Linda likes two dresses that she tries on. One dress costs $65.00. The other is $49.95. Which dress can Linda pay for by check? Circle your answer.

      $49.95 $65.00

Linda can use a check to pay for the $49.95 dress. The other dress costs more than Linda has left in her account. Her bank would not pay out more than Linda's balance.

Linda knows that it's important to look at her account balance before she writes a check. She always keeps her check register up to date.

Each time Linda writes a check, she fills in her register. She writes these things.

1. The check number _____

2. The date _____

3. The name of the person or place she paid

      _____

4. What she paid for

      _____

5. The amount of the check $_____

The last check she wrote had the number 006 printed at the top. Write that check number on the line by number 1.

Now, use Linda's check register to fill in the rest of the information about check number 006.

After Linda fills in those things, she figures out her new balance.

How much did Linda have in her account before she wrote the check to

Discount Village? $_____

Her balance was $83.20.

How did Linda figure out her new balance after writing the $25.00 check?

_____

_____

She *subtracted* the $25.00 from her old balance.

Linda decides to buy the $49.95 dress. She writes this check.

```
┌──────────────────────────────────────────────────────────────┐
│ LONGFIELD BANK                                    007    ◄──── Check
│ Longsfield, Missouri                                          number
│                         SAMPLE    May 27  19 97       81-7
│                                                        864
│ PAY TO THE ORDER OF   Donna's Dresses        $49.95
│   Forty-nine and 95/100                           DOLLARS
│
│ Linda DeGuzman
│ 625 River St.           Linda De Guzman
│ Longfield, Missouri 65804
│
│ ⑆86419766 2489 081796511 3377
└──────────────────────────────────────────────────────────────┘
```

Linda writes the information from the check in her register. The register is shown at the bottom of page 37.

Use Linda's check to fill in the information in her register. Under check number 006, write in the new check number.

The new number is 007.

Now, write the date in the next column.

The date on the check is May 27, 1997.

In the column marked *Description*, write the name of the store.

Linda shopped at *Donna's Dresses*.

Under the store name, write the name of the item Linda bought.

She bought a dress.

Write the amount in the *Withdrawal* column.

Linda paid $49.95 for her new dress.

Now, write -$49.95 in the *Balance* column. Subtract that amount from the $58.20.

Linda's new balance if $8.25.

$8.25 is not much of a balance. But Linda is not worried. She gets paid on May 28.

Linda deposits her paycheck. After she fills out her deposit slip, she brings her check register up to date.

In her register, Linda writes the date—May 28, 1997. Fill in that date in the *Date* column of the register below.

In the *Description* column, write **Deposit.** Under *Deposit,* write **paycheck.**

The amount of Linda's paycheck is $168.75. Write that amount in the column marked *Deposit*.

Now write $168.75 in the *Balance* column.

Add that deposit to the $8.25.

Linda's new balance is $177.00.

CHECK NUMBER	DATE	DESCRIPTION	AMOUNT OF WITHDRAWAL		AMOUNT OF DEPOSIT		BALANCE		
							$	83	20
006	May 19,	Discount Village	$	25	00	$		-25	00
	1997	radio						58	20

HELPFUL HINTS

A Always keep your check register up to date. Fill in your register each time you make a deposit or write a check.

B Add the amount of each deposit to your balance. The sum is your new balance.

C Subtract the amount of each check you write. The difference is your new balance.

D If your bank charges for each check you write, subtract the charge from your balance. Subtract any other service charges from your balance also. That way, you won't think you have more to spend than is left in your account.

E Your check register might have a very small place to write in the date. You have already learned one way to abbreviate the names of some months. Here's an even shorter way to write a date: 1/9/96.

The 1 stands for the first month of the year, January.

The 9 stands for the 9th day of the month.

The 96 stands for the year 1996.

1/9/96 stands for January 9, 1996.

Here are the numbers you can use to stand for the months of the year.

January—1	July—7
February—2	August—8
March—3	September—9
April—4	October—10
May—5	November—11
June—6	December—12

Try writing these dates the short way. The first one is done for you.

February 12, 1996 _2/12/96_____

September 5, 1997 _____

March 31, 1995 _____

June 27, 1999 _____

December 2, 1998 _____

PUZZLE TIME

Decide what word belongs in each blank. Then, find and circle that word in the puzzle. The answers are printed across, down, up, backwards, and on a slant.

1. A checkbook is also called a check _____.

2. The amount left in your account is your _____.

3. _____ the amount of each deposit to your balance.

4. _____ the amount of each check you write from your balance.

5. Subtract service _____ from your balance.

6. 10/6/97 stands for _____ 6th, 1997.

A	R	E	G	I	S	T	E	R	B
B	O	C	D	E	F	C	D	D	A
G	C	H	I	J	H	A	K	L	L
M	T	N	O	A	P	R	Q	R	A
S	O	T	R	U	V	T	W	X	N
Y	B	G	Z	A	B	B	C	D	C
E	E	F	G	H	I	U	J	K	E
S	R	L	M	N	O	S	P	Q	R

Reading Your Bank Statement

Andy has a checking account. One morning, the bank sends him a note. It says he has written a check for more money than he has in his account.

Andy phones Mr. Tom at the bank. "My checkbook shows that I have enough money," Andy says.

"You might have made a mistake adding or subtracting," Mr. Tom says. "Or the bank may have made a mistake in its own record. Did you read your **bank statement**?"

"Uh . . . no, I didn't," Andy says. "Would that help?"

"Yes," answers Mr. Tom. "The statement is the bank's record of your account. It helps you find out if your record is the same as the bank's. If the two records are not the same, there may be a mistake."

"What should I do now?" Andy asks.

"Bring me your check register and your bank statement," Mr. Tom says. "Let's find out what happened."

SECURITY BANK

CHECKING ACCOUNT #116-432615

Andy Johnson
110 Blake Avenue
Goldton, CA 94710

CHECKING ACCOUNT SUMMARY AS OF 03-26-97

BEGINNING BALANCE	TOTAL DEPOSITS	TOTAL WITHDRAWALS	SERVICE CHARGES	ENDING BALANCE
100.00	225.50	151.44	2.40	171.66

-------------------------- CHECKING ACCOUNT TRANSACTIONS --------------------------

DEPOSITS	DATE	AMOUNT
DEPOSIT	02-27	25.00
DEPOSIT	03-01	200.50
SERVICE CHARGES	03-26	2.40

CHECKS

ITEM	DATE	AMOUNT
001	02-29	23.41
002	03-07	60.66
003	03-14	48.78
004	03-21	18.59

BALANCES

DATE	BALANCE
02-27	125.00
02-29	101.59
03-01	302.09
03-07	241.43
03-14	192.65
03-21	174.06
03-26	171.66

At the bank, Mr. Tom explains each part of the statement to Andy. He tells Andy to read the top part first to make sure that his account number and address are right.

What is Andy's account number? Find it near the top of the statement. Write the number here.

_____

What town does Andy live in? Complete this line.

_____, CA 94710

THE MIDDLE PART OF THE STATEMENT

Mr. Tom and Andy look at the middle part of the bank statement next. It looks like this.

CHECKING ACCOUNT SUMMARY AS OF 03-23-97				
BEGINNING BALANCE	TOTAL DEPOSITS	TOTAL WITHDRAWALS	SERVICE CHARGES	ENDING BALANCE
100.00	225.50	151.44	2.40	171.66

The middle part gives a **summary** of Andy's account. The summary is a list of the most important facts in the statement.

The bank prepared Andy's account statement on March 26, 1997. Find and circle the date on the statement above.

The statement shows Andy's checking account summary as of 03-26-97. That's another way of writing March 26, 1997.

Andy's account summary shows these things.

1. **Beginning balance**—The amount of money in the account at the beginning of the month.

2. **Total deposits**—The sum of all the deposits Andy made during the month.

3. **Total withdrawals**—**Withdrawal** means "taking out." **Total Withdrawals** means the sum of all the checks Andy wrote.

4. **Service charges**—The bank charges Andy 60¢ for each check he writes. Sometimes the bank charges for other things too. The account summary shows the sum of all service charges during the month.

5. **Ending balance**—The amount of money in Andy's account on the day the statement is prepared.

Use the figures in Andy's account summary to answer these questions. The first one is done for you.

1. How much money did Andy have in his account at the beginning of the month? $___100.00___

2. How much money did Andy deposit during the month?

   $_____

3. How much money did the bank subtract from Andy's account to pay people who cashed Andy's checks? $_____

4. How much money did the bank charge Andy for services during the month? $_____

5. How much money did Andy have in his account on the day the statement was prepared? $_____

THE BOTTOM PART OF THE STATEMENT

All the things listed on the bottom part of Andy's statement are called **transactions.** A checking account transaction is anything that changes the account balance.

Look at Andy's checking account transactions on his statements below.

------------------------- CHECKING ACCOUNT TRANSACTIONS -------------------------

DEPOSITS			DATE	AMOUNT
DEPOSIT			02-27	25.00
DEPOSIT			03-01	200.50
SERVICE CHARGES			03-26	2.40

	CHECKS			BALANCES	
ITEM	DATE	AMOUNT		DATE	BALANCE
001	02-29	23.41		02-27	125.00
002	03-07	60.66		02-29	101.59
003	03-14	48.78		03-01	302.09
004	03-21	18.59		03-07	241.43
				03-14	192.65
				03-21	174.06
				03-26	171.66

How many deposits did Andy make?

_____

He made two deposits

How many checks did Andy write? _____

He wrote four checks.

One other type of transaction is listed. What is it?

_____

The bank subtracted service charges from Andy's account balance.

Deposits, checks, and service charges are three types of checking account transactions. After each transaction, the bank figures out Andy's new balance.

 # CANCELED CHECKS

When the bank sent Andy his account statement, it also sent his **canceled checks**.

Mr. Tom explains what a canceled check is. "When someone cashes a check you wrote, the bank pays the person the amount of money written on the check. The bank subtracts that amount from your account balance. Then the bank puts some markings on the back of the check to show that it has been cashed."

Andy and Mr. Tom go over Andy's statement, check register, receipts, and canceled checks. They discover a mistake. The bank forgot to add a deposit to Andy's account balance! Mr. Tom tells Andy that the bank will correct the mistake.

PUZZLE TIME

Look in the box for the word that belongs in each numbered sentence. Then write that word in the puzzle next to the matching number.

| balance |
| statement |
| canceled |
| transaction |
| summary |

1. Your checking account _____ is the bank's record of your account.

2. The checking account _____ is a list of the most important facts in the statement.

3. The ending _____ is the amount of money in your account on the day your statement is prepared.

4. A checking account _____ is anything that changes the account balance.

5. Your _____ checks are ones that have been cashed by the people you paid.

1. __ __ a __ __ __ __ __ __

2. __ __ __ __ a __ __

3. __ a __ __ __ __ __

4. __ __ a __ __ __ __ __ __ __ __

5. __ a __ __ __ __ __ __

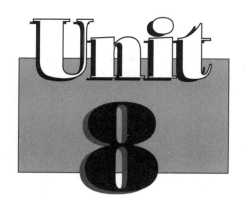

Balancing Your Check Register

Tony wants to buy a CB radio. He sees one he likes for $110.00. His check register shows a high enough balance. But the bank statement Tony just got shows too low a balance.

Tony knows that he can't write a check for more money than he has in his account. The bank wouldn't cash the check. And Tony would have to pay the bank $25.00 for his mistake.

Tony decides to balance his check register before he buys the CB radio. He will get his own record of his account to agree with the bank's record. Then his register will be balanced.

Tony's register is shown on page 47. Here's part of Tony's bank statement.

CHECKING ACCOUNT SUMMARY AS OF 07-29-97				
BEGINNING BALANCE	TOTAL DEPOSITS	TOTAL WITHDRAWALS	SERVICE CHARGES	ENDING BALANCE
43.24	101.13	38.87	1.35	104.15

First, Tony compares the ending balance on the bank statement with the *last* balance in his register. Write the two balances here.

Statement balance   Register balance

$_____ $_____

Tony sees that there is a big difference between the two balances. See if you can figure out why. Write your answer here.

_____

Did you notice that the two balances were figured out on different dates? Write the dates here.

Date statement prepared   Date of last register item

_____   _____

To balance his check register, Tony needs to compare the register balance and the statement balance for the *same* date. On the next few pages, you will see how he does this.

CHECK NUMBER	DATE	DESCRIPTION	AMOUNT OF WITHDRAWAL	AMOUNT OF DEPOSIT	BALANCE	
					$ 113	50
113	7/31/97	Cash	$ 25 00	$	-25	00
					88	50
	8/1/97	Deposit		76 13	+ 76	13
		Paycheck			164	63

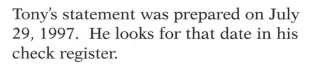

COMPARING DATES

Tony's statement was prepared on July 29, 1997. He looks for that date in his check register.

Tony's check register is shown on this page. Look down the *Date* column. Did Tony write anything in his register on July 29? Circle your answer.

Yes   No

No. Tony didn't use his check register on the date his statement was prepared. He looks for the last item *before* that date.

What was the date of the last register item before July 29?

July 23 is the answer. Tony draws a dark line under the July 23 item in his register.

Look at the last balance above the dark line in Tony's register.

Now, look at the ending balance on Tony's statement. The statement is shown on page 49.

Are the two balances the same?

Yes   No

No. Tony still has some figuring to do before he can balance his register.

CHECK NUMBER	DATE	DESCRIPTION	AMOUNT OF WITHDRAWAL		AMOUNT OF DEPOSIT		BALANCE $ 43 24	
	7/6/97	Deposit	$		$ 25	00	+ 25	00
		gift from mom & dad					68	24
110	7/15/97	Cash	15	00			- 15	00
							53	24
	7/18/97	Deposit			76	13	+ 76	13
		paycheck					129	37
111	7/20/97	Manny's Garage	23	87			- 23	87
		fix motorcycle					105	50
112	7/23/97	Snow Land	22	00			- 22	00
		ice show tickets					83	50
	7/30/97	Deposit			30	00	+ 30	00
		cleaning job					113	50
113	7/31/97	Cash	25	00			- 25	00
							88	50
	8/1/97	Deposit			76	13	+ 76	13
		paycheck					164	63

■ MARKING OFF TRANSACTIONS

The next thing Tony does is compare the checking account transactions shown on his statement with the items above the dark line in his register.

Tony finds the dates and amounts of his deposits and checks on his statement. Then, he marks off each of those items in his register.

Look at the part of Tony's bank statement shown below. What was the date of his first deposit?

On July 6, 1997, Tony deposited $25.00. Find Tony's record of that deposit in his register on page 48. Put an X next to the $25.00 in the *Deposit* column.

Now, put an X in the register next to each deposit and check that's listed on the statement.

CHECKING ACCOUNT SUMMARY AS OF 07-29-97

BEGINNING BALANCE	TOTAL DEPOSITS	TOTAL WITHDRAWALS	SERVICE CHARGES	ENDING BALANCE
43.24	101.13	38.87	1.35	104.15

-------------------------- CHECKING ACCOUNT TRANSACTIONS --------------------------

DEPOSITS	DATE	AMOUNT
DEPOSIT	07-06	25.00
DEPOSIT	07-18	76.13
SERVICE CHARGES	07-29	1.35

CHECKS

ITEM	DATE	AMOUNT
110	07-15	15.00
111	07-20	23.87

BRINGING THE STATEMENT UP TO DATE

Tony marked off in his register the deposits and checks listed on his statement.

There is one check listed above the dark line in Tony's register that is *not* marked off. Find that check in the register on this page. Write the amount of that check here.

$_____

Tony didn't mark off the $22.00 check to *Snow Land* because it isn't listed on his statement. We say it's an "outstanding" check.

Now, Tony knows that *Snow Land* has not cashed his check yet. But he also knows that he's already spent the $22.00. He needs to bring his statement up to date. To do that, he subtracts the amount of the outstanding check from the ending balance on the statement. Do the problem below.

$104.15   Ending balance on statement

- 22.00   Outstanding check

$ Final statement balance
          for July 29

The final statement balance is $82.15.

CHECK NUMBER	DATE	DESCRIPTION	AMOUNT OF WITHDRAWAL		AMOUNT OF DEPOSIT		BALANCE $ 43	24
	7/6/97	Deposit	$		$ X 25	00	+25	00
		gift from mom & dad					68	24
110	7/15/97	Cash	X 15	00			- 15	00
							53	24
	7/18/97	Deposit			X 76	13	+ 76	13
		paycheck					129	37
111	7/20/97	Manny's Garage	X 23	87			- 23	87
		fix motorcycle					105	50
112	7/23/97	Snow Land	22	00			- 22	00
		ice show tickets					83	50
	7/30/97	Deposit			30	00	+ 30	00
		cleaning job					113	50
113	7/31/97	Cash	25	00			- 25	00
							88	50
	8/1/97	Deposit			76	13	+ 76	13
		paycheck					164	63

There is one transaction listed on Tony's statement that is *not* in Tony's register. What is that transaction?

_____

The statement shows that $1.35 in service charges was taken out of Tony's account on July 29. That transaction is not listed in Tony's register.

Tony needs to bring his register up to date. To do that, he subtracts the $1.35 from the last register balance above the dark line.

Fill in the missing amount in the problem, then subtract.

$ Register balance above line

-   <u>1.35</u>   Service charges

$ Final register balance for July 29

$82.15 is the register balance after it has been brought up to date.

Now, compare Tony's final statement balance with his final register balance.

Statement	Register
$82.15	$82.15

The two amounts are the same for July 29. Tony's register is balanced. Tony is glad he balanced his check register before he bought the CB radio. He does not have enough money in his account to write a check for the CB radio.

CHECKING ACCOUNT SUMMARY AS OF 07-29-97

BEGINNING BALANCE	TOTAL DEPOSITS	TOTAL WITHDRAWALS	SERVICE CHARGES	ENDING BALANCE
43.24	101.13	38.87	1.35	104.15

-------------------------- CHECKING ACCOUNT TRANSACTIONS --------------------------

DEPOSITS	DATE	AMOUNT
DEPOSIT	07-06	25.00
DEPOSIT	07-18	76.13
SERVICE CHARGES	07-29	1.35

CHECKS

ITEM	DATE	AMOUNT
110	07-15	15.00
111	07-20	23.87

PUZZLE TIME

There is a word missing from each sentence clue below. Instead of the word, you will see the name of the place in the crossword puzzle where the word belongs.

Read clue number 1.

Find the word in the box on page 53 that belongs in place of **5-DOWN** in sentence number 1.

The answer is **agree**.

Find the puzzle squares for **5-DOWN**. Write in the word agree.

Now, do the rest of the puzzle the same way.

1. To balance your check register, you get your own record of your account to **5-DOWN** with the bank's record.

2. To balance your check register, you compare the register balance and the statement balance for the same **1-DOWN**.

3. You might not have used your register on the date your statement was prepared. Then you use the balance after the last item **6-ACROSS** that date.

4. In your register, you mark off each transaction listed on your **4-ACROSS.**

5. To bring your statement up to date, you subtract your outstanding **3-DOWN** from the ending balance.

6. To bring your register up to date, you subtract any **4-DOWN** charges from your balance.

7. If the final statement balance and the final register balance are the same, your register is **2-ACROSS.**

before

service

agree

checks

date

balanced

statement

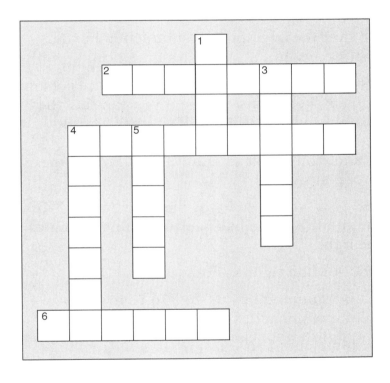

Help with Balancing Your Check Register

What can you do if your check register doesn't balance? This unit will show you three things to help you find and fix any mistakes.

A Go over the addition and subtraction in your check register.

It's easy to make a mistake in the balance column of your check register. See if you can find the mistake in balance column number 1 at the right. Go over each addition problem and subtraction problem. Draw a line through the wrong answer.

$58.24 is wrong. What is the right answer? Do the subtraction in balance column number 2 at the right.

$53.24 is the right answer.

Now, add the $53.24 to the $76.13 in balance column number 2.

The answer is $129.37.

Compare the last balance in column number 1 with the last balance in column number 2. Are they the same or different? Circle your answer.

Same   Different

They're different. When you correct any number in the balance column, you need to correct all the addition and subtraction after that number.

1 BALANCE

$ 43	24
+25	00
68	24
-15	00
58	24
+76	13
134	37

2 BALANCE

$ 43	24
+25	00
68	24
-15	00
+76	13

B Compare amounts on canceled checks with amounts in your register.

Suppose you had this list of canceled checks on your bank statement.

ITEM	DATE	AMOUNT
350	05-15	62.47
351	05-20	15.00

Now, suppose your check register looked like this.

CHECK NUMBER	DATE	DESCRIPTION	AMOUNT OF WITHDRAWAL	AMOUNT OF DEPOSIT	BALANCE	
					$ 150	00
350	5/15/97	Steve's Stereo	$ 66 47	$	- 66	47
		CD Player			83	53
351	5/20/97	Cash	15 00		- 68	53

Are the amounts on the statement the same as the amounts in the register? Circle your answer.

        Yes   No

No. For check number 350, the statement lists $62.47. But $66.47 is written in the register.

To find out which amount is right, you can look at your canceled checks and your receipts. If the mistake is in your register, you need to fix the amount in the withdrawal column and in the balance column. Then you need to figure out your new balance. Correct all the balances after the first one you fix.

If the mistake is on the statement, call your bank. The bank will fix its records.

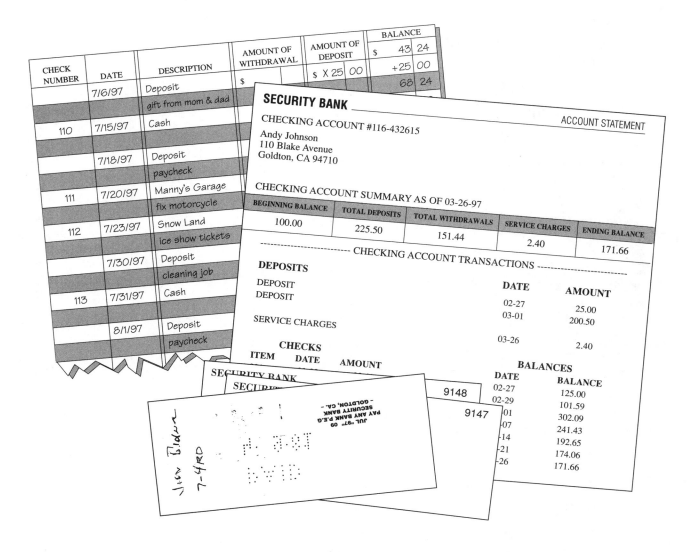

C Get help from your bank.

Suppose you cannot balance your check register and you cannot find any mistakes. Then you need to take four things to your bank:

> your bank statement;
> your receipts;
> your canceled checks; and
> your check register.

Someone at the bank will help you.

56

PUZZLE TIME

Look in the box for the word that belongs in each blank.
Then write in your answer.

If your check register doesn't balance, you can do these
things.

1. Go over the addition and subtraction in your check

   _____.

2. Correct any mistakes in the _____.
   column.

3. Correct all the addition and subtraction

   _____ the first correction.

4. Compare amounts on _____ checks
   with amounts in your register.

5. Fix any mistakes in the _____
   column and the balance column of your register.

6. Ask your bank to fix any mistakes on your

   _____.

7. If you can't find any mistakes, ask your

   _____ for help.

8. Compare amounts on your _____ to
   amounts in your register.

bank
canceled
register
statement
balance
after
withdrawal
receipts

◼ REVIEW TIME

How can you keep an eye on your money? The answer will appear at the bottom of page 59. But first you have to complete the puzzle.

Start by deciding what word is missing from each numbered sentence below. Then, write that word on the lines next to the matching number on page 59.

Read sentence number 1. Then look at the way the missing word is filled in on page 59.

Now, do numbers 2, 3, 4, and 5 the same way.

1. Another name for a checkbook is a check _____.

2. In the balance column of your check register, you add each deposit and _____ each check.

3. A checking account _____ is anything that changes the account balance, like a deposit, a check, or a service charge.

4. A _____ check is one that has been cashed and marked on the back by the bank.

5. _____ your check register means getting your register and the bank statement to agree.

1. <u>R</u> <u>E</u> <u>G</u> <u>I</u> <u>S</u> <u>T</u> <u>E</u> <u>R</u>
   6   1   7

2. __ __ __ __ __ __ __ __
       13   10 3   14

3. __ __ __ __ __ __ __ __ __ __ __
   16   15   12 18   9

4. __ __ __ __ __ __ __ __
   8 21 23   2 4 17 11

5. __ __ __ __ __ __ __ __ __
   20 22 5   19 24

Now, put each numbered letter from your answers into the message below. Write each letter above the line that has the matching number. You will find out how to keep an eye on your money!

<u>K</u> __ <u>P</u> __ __ __ __ __ __ __ __ __
   1 2   3 4 5   6 7 8 9 10 11 12

__ <u>P</u> __ <u>O</u> <u>D</u> __ __ __ __ __ <u>D</u>
13   14   15 16 17 18 19

__ __ <u>L</u> __ __ __ <u>E</u> <u>D</u> !
20 21   22 23 24

Using Your Checking Account

Lisa used to have trouble keeping track of her money. But now she has a checking account. She can find out how much money she has by looking in her check register. Her register also tells her *how* she's spending her money.

Lisa has learned how to make deposits and write checks. She has also learned how to keep her register up to date and how to balance her register with her bank statements.

When Lisa began paying for things by check, she also learned some other important things.

WHEN YOU CAN PAY BY CHECK

Lisa discovered that some places do not take checks. To buy something at those places, she must pay cash.

Before Lisa writes a check to pay for something, she asks the salesperson if the place will take a check.

SHOWING IDENTIFICATION

To pay with a check, Lisa must show some identification. Identification has your picture and your signature on it. If you do not have a driver's license, you might be able to get a special card from the same place people go to get a license.

Some banks give a special identification card to people who have checking accounts. The bank card shows your name, account number, and signature.

Most places will not accept student cards, library cards, or Social Security cards as identification.

KEEPING CANCELED CHECKS

Lisa uses her canceled checks for more than just balancing her check register. She uses them to prove she has paid for things she buys.

Once in a while, you may need to show someone that you paid money for something. You can do that by showing the person the canceled check. So do not throw away canceled checks. Keep them in a safe place.

Some banks don't return canceled checks. The checks are photographed and stored on film. The bank will make a copy of the check if you need to prove payment. You may need to pay a service charge for a copy of the check.

PUZZLER

Match the phrases to complete the sentences. Draw a line from the words on the left to the words on the right. The first pair is done for you.

1. You can find out how much money you have by
2. Before you write a check,
3. To pay by check, you must
4. A driver's license and a bank card are
5. You can use canceled checks

a. show some identification.
b. looking in your check register.
c. to prove that you paid for something.
d. two kinds of identification.
e. ask if the store will take a check instead of cash.

What happens to your money when you have a checking account? To find out, see what happens to one check in Lisa's account.

Lisa opens a checking account and deposits $100.00.

Lisa pays Mr. Ruiz $20.00 for some records. She pays by check.

Mr. Ruiz endorses Lisa's check. He gives the check to his bank. The teller gives Mr. Ruiz $20.00 in cash.

4

Mr. Ruiz's bank sends Lisa's $20.00 check to her bank.

5

Lisa's bank gives Mr. Ruiz's bank $20.00 out of Lisa's account.

6

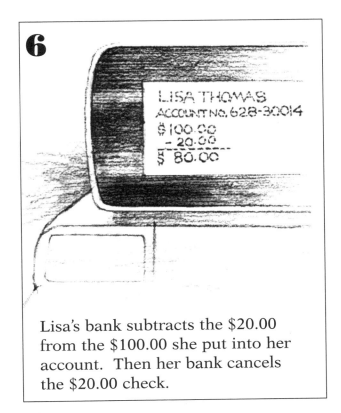

Lisa's bank subtracts the $20.00 from the $100.00 she put into her account. Then her bank cancels the $20.00 check.

7

Lisa's bank sends her a statement and the canceled $20.00 check. The statement shows that Lisa has $80.00 left.

CREDIT CHECK

There is a word missing from each sentence clue below. Instead of the word, you will see the name of the place in the crossword puzzle where the word belongs.

Decide what word belongs in each blank. Then write that word in its place in the puzzle.

1. Before you can pay for things by check, you must put **4-DOWN** into a checking account.

2. You can't write checks for more money than you have left in your **3-DOWN.**

3. The people you pay go to their banks to get **5-ACROSS** for your checks.

4. Your bank pays their **1-DOWN** cash for your checks.

5. Your bank **2-DOWN** the amounts on your checks from your account.

6. Your bank sends you your canceled checks with a **2-ACROSS** showing the bank's Record of your account.

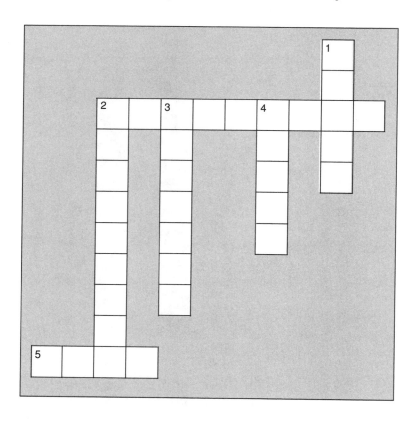